A GUIDE TO SOFT CLAY ART

CLAY ART
for special occasions

Yukiko Miyai

ISLAND HERITAGE™
PUBLISHING

ISLAND HERITAGE™
P U B L I S H I N G
A DIVISION OF THE MADDEN CORPORATION

94-411 KŌʻAKI STREET, WAIPAHU, HAWAIʻI 96797-2806
Orders: (800) 468-2800 • Information: (808) 564-8800
Fax: (808) 564-8877
islandheritage.com

ISBN: 1-59700-755-2
First Edition, Seventh Printing, 2016

Photography by: Roméo Collado

Acknowledgments

I am elated to share this unique clay art in a second series book. I've always dreamt of the opportunity to get the word out on clay art and the endless possibilities of what can be achieved with CLAYCRAFT by DECO.

Since my last book, *Clay Art for All Seasons*, I have wanted to share new techniques and designs. What I have achieved in this current book makes me extremely proud, and I am eternally grateful to so many fantastic colleagues, without whom none of this would be possible.

I wish to thank the following people…

Dale Madden of the Madden Corporation-for giving me the opportunity to publish this new book.

Scott Kaneshiro-your hard work and dedication to design is incredible.

Roméo Collado-your stunning photography captures my vision and makes this book beautiful.

Everyone at Island Heritage-it has been wonderful working with all of you. I appreciate you for letting me share my clay art.

My DECO Hawai'i team...Aya Yoshida-your superb editorial input and attention to detail are always appreciated.

Tim Janes-I am grateful for your encouragement, support, understanding, and giving me the gift of laughter.

Marlo Tajiri and Margaret Wong-I value your wholehearted and unending support throughout the years.

Mr. & Mrs. Gomes-for allowing us to use your lovely home as a backdrop for our photo shoot.

Erin Watson-for letting us capture your big, photogenic smile.

Stacey Nomura of Bradley & Lily Fine Stationery-for your support.

DECO Japan team-for supporting me during this past year.

My parents and family-especially to my Mother, Kazuko, my biggest inspiration, I truly look up to you as an artist.

Finally, thank you to all who have been a part of the DECO family. I truly am fortunate to have had the pleasure of teaching and getting to know you. Here's to many more years of clay art!

Yukiko Miyai

Table of Contents

Introduction

So much has changed since my first book, *Clay Art for All Seasons*, but some things haven't changed, and that is the pleasure and creative release that working with CLAYCRAFT™ by DECO® brings. For those already familiar with my first book, this second book is designed to provide more inspiration in the form of new projects and techniques to this ever-evolving art form. If you're new to decorative clay art, WELCOME! All the projects within the book have accompanying step-by-step photos and instructions that will have you, in no time, creating beautiful Clay Art for All Occasions!

Some background on CLAYCRAFT by DECO; this innovative air-dried modeling clay is ideal for the simplest projects to the most complex. It is light, pliable, easy to work with, holds fine detail, and has superb color blending capabilities. Finished pieces, when dry, are not only beautiful, lightweight, and soft to the touch, but also durable.

My Mother, Kazuko Miyai, developed this unique clay product in Japan. Not fully satisfied with commercially available clays, she began working with a chemist to develop clay that fulfilled her love for creating, and she succeeded. Since 1981, she has been doing presentations and holding workshops to share her love of clay art. She has authored more than twenty craft books, been featured in art magazines, and continues to develop and enhance her unique techniques with increasing detail, sophistication and complexity. Through exhibitions and workshops, she has certified more than two thousand instructors abroad.

After training under the tutelage of my Mother, in 2000 I brought CLAYCRAFT by DECO to Hawai'i and founded DECO Clay Craft Academy. Since then we have expanded throughout the state of Hawai'i as well as the mainland. Much of our success is due to sharing our passion for this unique and wonderful art form. For more information, please visit the DECO Clay Craft Academy website at www.decoclay.com.

Yukiko Miyai

Getting Started

BASIC MATERIALS AND TOOLS

CLAYCRAFT by DECO soft clay comes in seven colors—white, red, yellow, blue, black, green, and brown. These basic colors can be mixed to create the exact colors you want for your own unique creations. See Color Chart on page 14 for mixing guidelines.

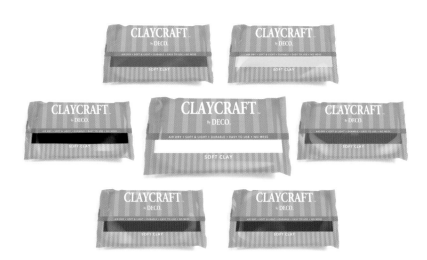

BASIC TOOLS

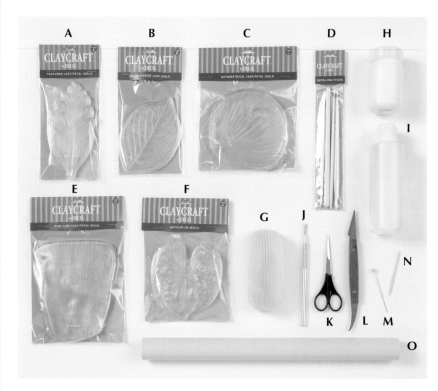

A CLAYCRAFT by DECO Textured Leaf/Petal Mold Type A – To make leaves and petals

B CLAYCRAFT by DECO Smooth Edge Leaf Mold Type B – To make leaves and petals

C CLAYCRAFT by DECO Asymmetrical Leaf/Petal Mold Type C – To make leaves and petals

D CLAYCRAFT by DECO Detailing Sticks Set – To create petals and texture

E CLAYCRAFT by DECO Fine Line/Petal Mold Type D – To make leaves and petals

F CLAYCRAFT by DECO Anthurium Mold Type E – To make leaves

G Plastic Texture Brush – To add texture to clay

H White Glue – To attach clay pieces to other materials

I Water Glue – For clay on clay attachment

J Texture Brush – To add lines, marks or texture

K Scissors – To cut off excess clay, cut and separate petals and for detail

L Ryoba Cutter – To cut the clay

M Pin – For intricate details such as patterns on the clay surface

N Toothpick – To roll out small petals

O Roller – To flatten and stretch the clay

ADDITIONAL TOOLS AND MATERIALS

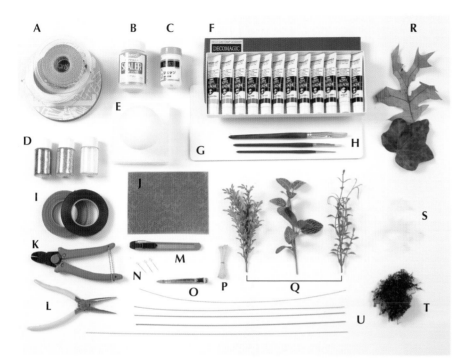

A   Ribbons – Used as a finishing touch to your projects

B   Semi-gloss Varnish – To add shine to your pieces

C   White Gesso – To mix with acrylic paints

D   Glitters – To add accents to your pieces

E   Styrofoam forms – Used as a base for large projects

F   DECO Acrylic Set – To add accents to your pieces

G   Palette – Surface to mix DECO Acrylic paints

H   DECO Paintbrushes (sizes 0, 6, 12) – Used with DECO Acrylic Set

I   Floral Tape – To cover exposed wires attached to some flowers

J   Printmaker – To make patterns on clay

K   Wire Cutter – To cut wires

L   Long Nose Pliers – To arrange flowers in tight spaces

M   Box Cutter – To cut Styrofoam and thick pieces of dried clay

N   Corsage Pins – To secure ribbons

O   Hair Clip – Used as a base to make arrangements for hair

P   Artificial Stamen – For use with some flowers

Q   Plastic Green Fillers – To add accents or fill gaps in arrangements

R   Plastic Leaves – To add accents to your arrangements

S   Feathers – To add accents to birds

T   Moss – To add accents to your arrangements

U   Floral Wires – used to make stems, hair picks and for arrangements

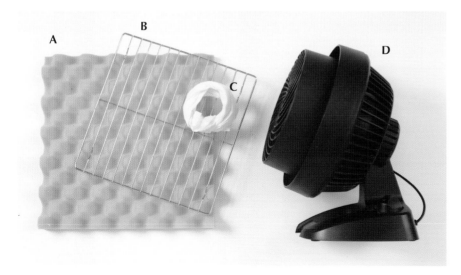

A   Drying Foam – Used as a soft surface to dry flowers

B   Cooling Rack – Used to dry flowers with large petals

C   Paper Towel Ring – Used to dry flowers with large or long petals

D   Fan – Used to dry flowers

WORKING WITH THE CLAY

Follow these simple guidelines to make working with CLAYCRAFT by DECO easy:

- Begin by briefly kneading the clay between your fingers to soften it.
  (Be sure not to over-knead as this can make the clay too stiff.)
- Work on a flat, non-absorbent surface that will preserve the clay's moisture.
- If the clay becomes too dry, add a little fresh, soft clay, or a few drops of water to restore its softness and pliability.
- As you finish the various sections of your piece, keep them moist so they will stick together during final assembly.
  Do this by moistening paper towels and covering your unused clay and "parts" of your unfinished projects.
- Air-dry your completed item. The average drying times are half a day for the outer surface and one to two days for the item to dry completely, although this can vary according to climate. Depending on the size and shape of the item, you can set items to dry on paper towels tied into rings, bumpy-surfaced sponges, metal baking racks, or egg cartons.
- If desired, you may add paint to your finished item, or you may brush on a light coat of varnish to add sheen and prevent discoloration.
- Wrap leftover clay, including color-mixed clay, in a damp paper towel and keep in an airtight container or plastic bag, or wrap tightly in plastic wrap.

BASIC TECHNIQUES

Large balls: Roll the amount you will need on your work surface with the palm of your hand.

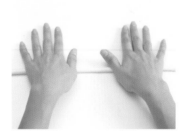

Ropes: Start with a ball and roll it back and forth with both hands to stretch it to the thickness you need.

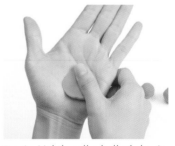

Petals: Lightly roll a ball of clay in the palm of your hand, then press the ball with your thumb to the desired petal shape.

Flattening the clay: Use your roller to flatten the clay to the thickness you need, the same way you roll out dough.

"Ruffling" clay: Roll out the clay with one side thinner than the other. On the thinner side, use fingers to pull and then twist the clay.

Color mixing: To mix colors, pull and stretch the clay to get your colors mixed well. This is almost like stretching taffy.

BASIC LEAF

1 Using the base of your palm, roll a 1-inch diameter ball of green clay into a 1-inch teardrop.

2 Press teardrop onto textured side of leaf mold, pointing tip of leaf upward.
3 Spread clay to desired size and shape.

4 Detach beginning at wide end; grooves will be impressed onto clay.
5 Slightly twist and bend sides to give desired shape and form.

STEM

1 Roll 2-inch diameter ball of green clay into a 6-inch long rope.

2 Press #18-gauge wire into middle of rope.

3 Pinch top of clay around wire.

4 Starting from middle of wire, gently press and roll out clay, moving your hands out from middle to stretch clay. Continue rolling until wire is completely covered.

ATTACHING STEM TO FLOWER

1 Cut about 1-inch of clay off one end of wire. Stem should be completely dried.

2 Add glue to exposed wire and insert into dry flower.
3 Add a little clay to area where flower meets stem to finish.

COLOR MIXING

The Color Chart shows basic colors and proportions to use to achieve various colors for your projects. When making new colors, estimate the amount you'll need and then add colors in very small amounts as you knead the clay to get the exact shade you want.

For pastels, mix just a tiny pinch of colored clay into white clay.

PRIMARY

yellow + blue + black = green

yellow + red + black = brown

red + yellow = true red

red + yellow + black = maroon

yellow + red = orange

red + blue = purple

PASTELS

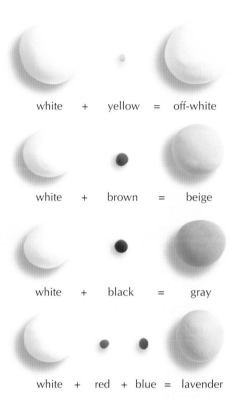

white   +   yellow   =   off-white

white   +   brown   =   beige

white   +   black   =   gray

white   +   red   +   blue   =   lavender

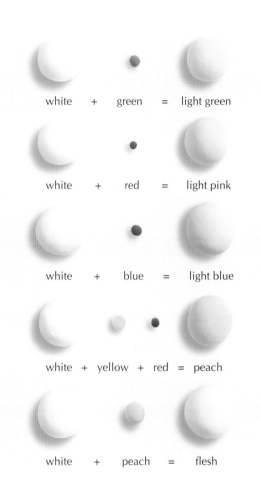

white   +   green   =   light green

white   +   red   =   light pink

white   +   blue   =   light blue

white   +   yellow   +   red   =   peach

white   +   peach   =   flesh

Bridal Shower

Cherry Blossoms

TOOLS & SPECIAL MATERIALS

Flower:
Scissors
Toothpick
Artificial Stamens
White Glue

Assembly:
Stem (see pg.13)
#24 Gauge Wire
#28 Gauge Wire
Floral Tape (Brown)
White Glue

CHERRY BLOSSOMS

CHERRY BLOSSOMS

1 Cut one ¾-inch teardrop making larger end of teardrop slightly off center. Cut smaller piece in half and large piece into three parts to make five petals.

2 Squeeze neck area to open cut portions.

3 With index finger at base, gently roll out each section with toothpick to form petals. If sides of petals stick to each other, separate with scissors.

4 Cut out a tiny "v" on each petal.

5 Cut sides of petals to separate from each other.

6 Cut stamen to ½-inch. Glue end of stamen and insert into center.

ASSEMBLY

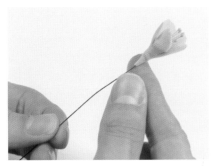

1 Take excess clay at base and glue end of 3-inch long #28 wire and insert into base of flower. Pull extra clay ½-inch down and around stem. Let dry and wrap each stem with floral tape.

2 Cluster 4-5 dried flowers and secure with floral tape. To make bud, wrap #24 gauge wire with floral tape and add green clay on one end.

3 Wrap main stem with floral tape.

4 Attach buds and flowers on main stem with floral tape.

5 To make a longer branch, make a longer stem in the beginning.

Peony

TOOLS & SPECIAL MATERIALS

Mold D
Stem (see pg.13)
Toothpick
White Glue

PEONY

PEONY

NOTE:
As the balls are created, place a damp paper towel underneath and over them.

1 Make fifteen ½-inch, ten ¾-inch and ten 1-inch diameter balls, a 3~4 inch stem (used only for support), and a 12~13 inch stem (see page 13).

2 Form balls into teardrops. Using mold D, press top and edge of the petals thin, gradually leaving middle to the bottom areas thicker.

3 Use toothpick to make a few incisions.

4 Press and stretch edges to make petals thinner.

5 Use fingers to slightly pull edges.

6 With petal in cup of your hand, press middle with finger to curve petal inward.

7 Make 1-inch long teardrop and put larger end on shorter stem. Make sure that the stem goes all the way to the top of the teardrop.

CALYX

8 Wrap by rolling the petal inward, higher than its center, and overlapping one-third of the petal (as pictured) to make bud.

9 Attach middle petals, keeping it at same height as the bud. Continue to attach remaining large petals, place last five petals slightly lower.

10 When finished, take stem out. Tear away excess clay at base. Let flower dry completely before putting calyx.

1 Make five 1 ½-inch and three 1 ¼-inch long teardrops.

2 Make five teardrops like petals. Press three teardrops on mold D to make them longer and thinner on top.

3 Apply glue to the base of the wider calyx and adhere to flower.

4 Repeat with longer calyx and place between wider calyxes.

5 Smooth bottom and cut about ¾-inch of clay from stem to expose wire. Apply white glue, insert stem and tear away excess at base. Cut stem to desired length.

Weddings

Ranunculus

TOOLS & SPECIAL MATERIALS

Assembly:
Stem (see pg.13)
#20 Gauge Wire
White Glue
Floral Tape (Green)
Green Fillers
Wire Cutter
Ribbons
Corsage Pins

RANUNCULUS

RANUNCULUS

NOTE:

As the balls are created, place a damp paper towel underneath and over them.

1 Make one ½-inch diameter ball for center, fifteen ⅜-inch (small), ten ½-inch (medium) and ten ¾-inch (large) diameter balls.

2 Use rounded base of your palm to roll ball into teardrop.

3 Place large end of teardrop in your palm, then press and spread top of clay thin to form petal. Leave last ten petals thicker than rest.

4 Use ½-inch ball to make teardrop for the center. Place three small petals around the larger end and slightly higher than center.

5 Layer center with colors that gradually get lighter. Continue overlapping half of small petals, placing on top first. Holding the bottom of the petal with left thumb, stretch right side.

6 Repeat with medium petals, placing on top first. Hold petal with left thumb and stretch right side as petal is placed.

7 Repeat with first five large petals placing on top first. Stretch less to the sides.

ASSEMBLY

8 For the last five large petals, place petals lower from the bottom and stretch petals to the side to make them look more opened.

9 Tear away any excess clay at base and let it dry.

1 Cut about ¾-inch of clay from stem to expose wire. Apply glue and insert into dried flowers.

2 Make other flowers for arrangement. Attach stems to flowers. Use #20 gauge wire for green fillers and wrap with floral tape.

3 Cluster three large flowers and secure stems with floral tape. Keep adding flowers in between at same height until outer edge is reached.

4 Insert small flowers and fillers to fill gaps. Occasionally wrap stems with floral tape. Place fillers at the base to cover stems.

5 Cut bottom to of all wires to make length even.

6 Use floral tape to wrap area that will be covered with ribbon.

7 Wrap ribbon from bottom.

8 Fold end of ribbon and secure with corsage pins.

Tuberose
& Rose

TOOLS & SPECIAL MATERIALS

Flowers:
Mold D
DECO Detail Stick (Round)
Scissors
Toothpick

Assembly:
Mold B
White Glue
#20 Gauge Wire
Floral Tape (Green)
Ribbon

TUBEROSE AND ROSE

TUBEROSE

1 Make one ½-inch; for center, three ¼-inch (small), three ⅜-inch (medium) and six less than ½-inch (large) diameter balls.

2 Form narrow and long teardrops.

3 Press teardrop onto mold D and flatten top portion.

4 Peel clay from mold. Using index finger as base, gently press edges using round DECO detail stick.

5 Create cup shape by rolling tip of round DECO detail stick over petal.

6 To make center, cut teardrop into six equal parts.

7 With index finger at base, use toothpick to flatten cut sides.

8 Take every other petal and bring towards center.

TUBEROSE BUDS

9 Attach three small petals in between gaps, slightly higher than center.

10 Attach three more petals in between gaps, slightly higher than previous row. Continue with remaining six petals.

11 Stretch and smooth base and tear away any excess clay at base.

1 Make three ¼-inch diameter balls; roll into pointy teardrops. Also make five medium and five large pointy teardrops, gradually increasing in size.

ROSE

2 Stick three small pointy tear drops together.

3 Attach rest of pointed teardrops lower than first three.

1 Make three ¾-inch (small) and fifteen 1 inch (large) diameter balls.

2 Press each ball with your thumb to form petal shape. Make small petals extra thin around edges.

3 To create center, overlap three petals, about $1/16$-inch lower than previous petal. Roll petals together at base.

4 Roll left side to the center.

5 Wrap right side over.

6 Attach petal and wrap around center, keeping height of petals even.

7 Attach next petal opposite side of previous petal. Continue attaching petals by covering half of previous petal.

8 Attach remaining petals one at a time the same way, overlapping each at halfway point of previous petal. Flare last petal completely so entire petal curves out.

9 Calyx - Make five $1/2$-inch diameter balls; form into $1\ 1/4$-inch teardrops and flatten with palms of hands. Attach calyx leaves so they surround rose, with tips at the same height as petal tops.

10 Tear away excess at base.

ASSEMBLY

1 Apply glue to three inch long #20 gauge wire and insert into base of rose. Pull extra clay about ½-inch down and around stem and let dry.

2 Make 2 leaves.

3 Apply glue to one end of three inch long #20 gauge wire and push one-third of way into middle of leaf. Pull extra clay about ½-inch down and around stem and let dry.

4 Attach wires and wrap floral tape to each piece.

5 Cluster rose, three tuberoses and buds. Wrap with floral tape.

6 Place leaves and fillers. Secure with floral tape.

7 Wrap ribbon from bottom. Glue end.

Hydrangea

TOOLS & SPECIAL MATERIALS

Flower:
Scissors
Toothpick
DECO Detail Stick (Angled)
White Glue
#28 Gauge Wire
Floral Tape (Green)

Assembly:
Floral Tape (Green)
Styrofoam
Box Cutter
Roller
#18 Gauge Wire
#24 Gauge Wire
Stem (see pg.13)
Artificial Leaves
White Glue

HYDRANGEA

HYDRANGEA

1 Make ⅝-inch diameter ball; form into 1 ½-inch teardrop.

2 Cut larger end of teardrop into four equal parts, ½-inch deep.

3 Squeeze neck area to open cut parts.

4 Push down tips gently with finger.

5 With index finger at base, gently roll out top of each section with toothpick to form petals.

6 Cut side of petals to separate from each other.

7 Use angled DECO detail stick to add texture to flower.

8 Gently pull and twist tips.

9 Use slightly lighter or darker colored clay to make tiny teardrop.

10 Use toothpick to pick up tiny teardrop and insert in center of flower.

35

ASSEMBLY

11 Tear away excess clay at base.

12 Glue end of 2 inch length #28 wire and insert into base of flower. Pull extra clay ½-inch down and around stem. Let dry and wrap each wire with floral tape.

1 Cluster four flowers together and secure with floral tape. Add 1 ½-inch long #18 gauge wire and wrap with floral tape.

2 Cut Styrofoam to bag shape/trapezoid.

3 Use roller to flatten similar shade clay and cover Styrofoam.

4 Smooth clay.

5 Apply glue to the wires and insert clusters into covered Styrofoam.

6 Use #24 gauge wire to secure leaves to cover back.

7 (Picture of back)

8 Cover #18 gauge wire with white clay and let it dry. Wrap floral tape and cover with ribbon. Apply glue and insert both sides of stem into the top of the Styrofoam to create handle.

Gardenia

TOOLS & SPECIAL MATERIALS

Mold B
#18 Gauge Wire

GARDENIA

GARDENIA

1 Make five ¾-inch (small) and twelve 1-inch (large) diameter balls.

2 Form five 2-inch and twelve 2 ¼-inch long teardrops.

3 Place large end of teardrop in your palm, then press and spread top and edge of the petals thin gradually leaving middle and bottom areas thicker.

4 Remove petal from hand. With petal in cup of your hand, press middle with finger to curve petal inward.

5 Fan five small petals, cup face up, overlapping each about two-thirds over previous petal.

6 Roll left side towards center.

7 Wrap right side over left side.

8 Squeeze neck area to secure petals.

9 Add first six large petals at the same height with cup shape turned inward, overlapping one-third.

10 Hold petal with left thumb. Stretch right side as petal is placed.

11 For last six large petals, flip petals so that cup shape faces outward. Place about ¾-inch above center, right next to each other.

12 Press with knuckle to secure petals.

13 Slightly stretch outer petals and fold tips slightly together.

14 Open petals.

15 When dried, attach #18 gauge wire and arrange flowers and leaves as desired.

Baby Shower

Shoes

TOOLS & SPECIAL MATERIALS

Pattern
Roller
Ryoba Cutter
White Glue
Toothpick
Ribbon
Scissors

SHOES

SHOES

1 Roll clay ⅛-inch thick.

2 Apply white glue to copy of patterns (see page 86) and place over clay. Patterns will be used as support. Use ryoba cutter to cut clay around the patterns.

3 Attach front section of shoes to the base with glue.

4 Attach rest of patterns.

5 Make an 11-inch long strip to wrap around the base of shoe.

6 Attach sides of shoes made with a different color.

7 Trim excess clay.

8 Insert toothpick to make holes for shoelace.

9 Make stitch design by using toothpick. Repeat on other side.

10 When shoe dries, add shoelace/ribbon.

Butterfly

TOOLS & SPECIAL MATERIALS

Card
Ribbon
Pattern
Printmaker
Roller
DECO Detail Stick (Angled)
#28 Gauge Wire
White Glue
Glitter
Water Glue
Brush
Paint

BUTTERFLY

1 Roll out clay to ⅛-inch thick. Place printmaker over rolled out clay and use roller to imprint pattern.

2 Remove printmaker.

3 Freehand or use pattern (see page 87) with angled DECO detail stick and make as many butterflies that can fit on the clay.

4 Peel off excess clay and move butterfly to cardboard.

5 Create details by cutting holes in the wings.

6 Attach body of butterfly and let it dry. Put something heavy, such as a book, onto clay pieced when drying to prevent them from curling.

7 Glue ribbon on card and arrange butterfly. If desired, paint and add glitter by mixing with water glue and brush onto butterfly. Add antenna using #28 gauge wire.

Spring

Basket

TOOLS & SPECIAL MATERIALS

Bowl/container used to
    make basket shape
Roller
#18 Gauge Wire
White Glue
Scissors

BASKET

BASKET

NOTE:

To make basket, you will need a base container (such as paper box, ceramic or plastic) that is smooth. If clay dries, ropes will not attach together and will crack and break easily. Be sure to keep rope in between damp paper towel or cloth towel to keep moist.

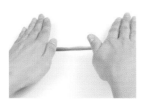

1 Make 40-50 ropes about 11-inches long and ⅛-inch thick. Place ropes between damp paper towel to prevent drying.

2 Lay odd number of ropes vertical and parallel to each other on top of a container.

3 Place one rope perpendicular in the middle.

4 Place vertical ropes over the one horizontal rope, but in between previous vertical ropes.

5 Lift all bottom vertical ropes over the horizontal rope.

6 Place a single horizontal rope below the first horizontal rope

7 Bring down the lifted vertical ropes to their original positions. Repeat steps 5-7 to add more horizontal ropes.

8 Add rope on the sides by placing ropes up and down.

9 When the rope makes a circle, connect at the bottom so the linked section is not visible.

10 Continue to add ropes until desired height is reached.

11 Trim off excess and let basket dry completely.

12 Make two 2-feet ropes about 3/16-inch thick. (Length will depend on the size of basket.) Place palms at each end. Twist clay, moving one hand forward and the other back, two or three times to make rope tight.

13 After basket is dried, remove from container. Use glue and attach rope made in step 12. Cut end of rope at an angle to make it look connected.

14 Make four 1-foot ropes about 3/16-inch thick. Bring top end together. Take rope farthest to the right and move it to the left, going up and down three ropes. Continue all the way.

15 Make one rope about 1-foot long and flatten with roller.

16 Insert #18 gauge wire between braided rope in step 14 and flat rope in step 15.

17 Bend ends to create handle. Cut to desired length, but expose about 1-inch of wire.

18 Apply white glue to wire and insert into basket.

19 Put rope to secure and cover connected areas. Add designs such as flowers and ribbons.

Bird
Ornament

TOOLS & SPECIAL MATERIALS

Scissors
Paint
Brush
Feathers

BIRD ORNAMENT

BIRD

1 Form two inch ball into teardrop shape.

2 Squeeze bigger section to make head.

3 Use finger to curl tip of tail.

4 Form three ⅝-inch balls into teardrops. One teardrop will be longer and skinnier than other two. Flatten all with palm.

5 Make slits on the edges of the two wings.

6 Attach wings to the sides of the body.

7 Make longer slits for the back tail and attach to the bottom.

8 Make tiny teardrop. Attach larger portion to the mouth area to make beak. Form beak shape with fingers.

9 Make eye areas by using opening of retractable pen.

10 Attach bird feathers on top of clay wings.

11 Attach bird feather on top of the tail.

12 Use longer feather and attach to bottom of clay tail.

13 Paint eyes with black paint. Paint body as desired.

Poppy & Freesia

TOOLS & SPECIAL MATERIALS

Flower:
DECO Detail Stick
  (Angled and Round)
Plastic Texture Brush
Artificial Stamens
Mold D
Toothpick
White Glue

Assembly:
Styrofoam
White Glue
Container
#18 Gauge Wire
Green Fillers

POPPY AND FREESIA

POPPY CENTER

1 To make center, roll 1-inch diameter ball into pointed teardrop and make five lines using angled DECO detail stick.

2 Insert angled DECO detail stick to the tip to create a hole.

3 Use plastic brush to add texture all over.

4 Cut stamen to ⅝-inch long. Glue end of stamen and attach to center a few at a time.

POPPY PETALS

1 Make six 2-inch long (small) and eight 2 ½-inch long (large) teardrops.

2 Using mold D, press top and edge of the petals thin gradually leaving middle to the bottom areas thicker.

3 With index finger at base, gently roll angled DECO detail stick on the edges of each petal.

4 With petal in cup of your hand, press middle with knuckle to curve petal inward.

FREESIA

5 Wrap six petals around center. Keep same height, slightly overlap each other. Last petal will go inside of the first petal.

6 Place remaining eight petals slightly higher. Take away excess clay at base and let flower dry.

1 Roll three ½-inch and three ¾-inch diameter balls into pointed teardrops.

2 Flatten top portion by placing on mold D.

3 Use round DECO detail stick to smooth edges.

4 Assemble three smaller petals in fan shape, keeping distance far from each other.

5 Roll left side towards center and wrap right side close to the left petal.

6 Use angled DECO detail stick to open center.

7 Slightly cup three petals and place then in between first three petals.

8 Squeeze bottom and tear away excess at bottom.

9 Open center again with angled DECO detail stick.

10 Make four to five skinny stamens.

ASSEMBLY

11 Bundle together.

12 Use toothpick to pick up stamen and insert in center of flower.

1 Arrangement - To arrange flowers, cover Styrofoam with green clay. Apply glue to the bottom and press onto container. Use white glue and attach #18 gauge wire to dried flowers.

2 Use white glue and place first flower, usually the biggest, in the center. Arrange flowers around the first flower.

3 Fill gaps with smaller flowers and fillers.

Summer

Cymbidium Orchid

TOOLS & SPECIAL MATERIALS

Flower:
Stem (see pg.13)
White Glue
Water Glue
Toothpick
Mold D
DECO Detail Stick (Round)
Scissors

Paint and Assembly:
Paint
Brush (#0 and 6)
Palette
White Glue
#18 Gauge Wire

CYMBIDIUM ORCHID

CYMBIDIUM ORCHID

1 Make five 1-inch diameter balls for petals, one ¾-inch for stamen and one 1-inch diameter ball for center. Prepare 2-inch long stem.

2 For column and lip, form ball into skinny and fat teardrop. For petals, make pointed teardrops.

3 Column – Press teardrop in between palm of hands.

4 Cup center by pressing gently with index finger and tear away excess at bottom.

5 Cut to expose about ½-inch of wire from stem. Glue end of wire and insert into base of center. Smooth base to connect with stem.

LIP

1 Press edges of lip on a flat surface.

2 Use toothpick to make few incisions.

3 Press and spread edges with fingers leaving middle to the bottom areas thicker.

4 Place lip in cup of your hand and press center with your index finger to curve it inward. Cut 1-inch of tail of lip

5 Apply water glue or white glue to lip and wrap around column to form stamen.

6 Let stamen dry in front of fan.

PETALS

1 Use mold D to flatten petals leaving middle to the bottom areas thicker.

2 Use round DECO detail stick to smooth edges.

3 Gently cup petals with finger.

4 Trim bottom of each petal at an angle.

PAINT AND ASSEMBLY

5 Apply water glue or white glue to petals. Attach first two petals on both sides of lip.

6 Attach one petal between the two petals. Attach two remaining petals between petals and lip, then evenly spread out petals. Smooth bottom and let it dry.

1 Paint when flowers are completely dried. Prepare white gesso, red, purple and yellow paints. Mix white gesso, red and yellow to make peach color. Using dried brush, paint edges of lip and center.

2 Add darker peach color on edges.

3 Mix red and purple and paint edges and dot lips.

4 See page 57 for arrangement instructions.

Anthurium

TOOLS & SPECIAL MATERIALS

Flower:
Roller
Mold E
Scissors
Plastic Texture Brush
DECO Detail Stick (Angled)

Paint and Assembly:
Stem (see pg.13)
Paint
Brush (#6 and 12)
Palette
Semi-gloss varnish
Styrofoam Ball
Moss Sheet
Mold D
#20 Gauge Wire
DECO Detail Stick (Angled)
White Glue
Plate

ANTHURIUM

ANTHURIUM

1 Prepare 3-inch diameter ball formed into teardrop and 2-inch long rope. Make light green skinny stem.

2 Using roller, flatten teardrop to $1/16$-inch thick.

3 Cut clay into heart shape.

4 Place heart shape on Mold E.

5 Press clay into grids of the mold.

6 Peel clay out of the mold and trim excess.

7 Place cut out onto the mold again. Repeat steps 5 and 6 to obtain desired thickness and detail.

8 Press on mold and leave to dry.

9 Use palm of hand to roll out flower, about two inches long.

10 Use plastic brush to add texture.

PAINT AND ASSEMBLY

11 Slightly bend the tip and let it dry.

1 Colors used are: white gesso, purple, orange, rose, green and yellow. Mix white gesso and red to make pink color. With dry brush, paint front and back of leaf. Add darker pink and highlight areas shown in picture.

2 Mix lighter pink and blend dark areas. Make light green by mixing white gesso, green and yellow and use dry brush to accent a few areas.

3 Color both edges of flower with light green mixture using dry brush.

4 Apply varnish to bring out gloss to anthurium and flower. Repeat coating as needed.

5 Expose ¼-inch wire of the stem. Apply glue and insert wire through back of anthurium.

6 Apply glue to base of flower and insert into wire.

7 Use mold D to make leaf. Run angled DECO detail stick through the middle. Apply glue to 2 ½-inch long #20 gauge wire and insert into leaf. Leave out 1 ½-inch of wire.

8 Glue back of moss sheet and cover Styrofoam ball. Apply glue to plate, add clay, apply glue and stick moss ball on top.

9 Attach dried leaf. Apply glue to stem with anthurium and insert into moss ball.

Torch Ginger

TOOLS & SPECIAL MATERIALS

Flower:
DECO Detail Stick (Round)
Stem (see pg.13)

Assembly:
Clip
Hot Glue
White Glue
Green Fillers

TORCH GINGER

TORCH GINGER

1 Make ten ½-inch and eight ¾-inch diameter balls into pointed teardrops. Prepare 3-inch long stem.

2 Press teardrop in palm of hand to flatten.

3 Flatten teardrop with fingertips to form petal.

4 Use round DECO detail stick to smooth edges.

5 With petal in cup of your hand, press middle with finger to curve petal inward.

6 Apply small amount of clay on top of dried 3-inch stem.

7 Wrap first petal above center.

8 Add two more petals to cover center. Continue wrapping seven petals, overlapping one-third of previous petals. Make sure they are the same height.

ASSEMBLY

9 For the remaining eight petals, overlap one-fourth of previous petal and place slightly lower.

10 Place last petal and gently squeeze base to open petals.

11 Stretch and tear away excess clay at base. After flower dries, cut exposed stem.

1 Attach plastic green leaves onto clip using hot glue.

2 Apply white glue underneath green clay.

3 Arrange big flowers first. Using white glue.

4 Add smaller flowers and fillers.

Dahlia

TOOLS & SPECIAL MATERIALS

Flower and Leaf:
Scissors
DECO Detail Stick (Angled)
Mold D
Mold C
Pattern
White Glue
#20 Gauge Wire

Assembly:
Styrofoam
Toothpick
White Glue
Plastic Leaves
Scissors
#18 Gauge Wire

D A H L I A

DAHLIA

1 Roll ¼, ⅜ and ½-inch diameter balls in light, medium and dark colors respectively. Make twenty 1-inch long, twenty 1 ½-inch long and thirty 2-inch long and pointed teardrops. Make three 1-inch diameter balls for center.

2 Flatten teardrop using Mold D. Peel clay from mold. Using index finger as base, gently press edges using angled DECO detail stick and roll out edges, leaving the bottom half thicker than top half.

3 Form three 1-inch diameter balls into pointed teardrops and make a cut in the middle ⅝-inch deep. Continue cutting multiple times all around.

4 Bunch one of the cut parts together.

5 For second and third balls, make into pointed teardrops and cut multiple times like in previous step. Cut open in half.

6 Wrap clay from step 4 around center.

7 Repeat steps 5 and 6 for third ball and wrap around center.

8 Attach small petals to the center, keeping all the same height, and leave spaces in between each other. Continue placing small petals in between gaps.

9 Before placing medium petals, pinch base of petals. Place medium petals at the same height but slightly higher than small petals.

LEAF

10 Continue with large petals, going slightly higher than medium petals.

11 Tear away excess at bottom and let it dry.

1 Roll out clay and cut leaf shape using pattern (see page 87).

2 Press cut out leaf on mold C.

3 Take out clay from mold and place textured leaf side up. Use tip of angled DECO detail stick to add thicker veins on each leaf.

ASSEMBLY

4 Make different shape leaves.

5 Apply white glue to 3-inch long #20 gauge wire and insert into base of leaf. To secure base, twist clay down and around wire. Paint to desired colors when dried.

1 Cut Styrofoam to make cylinder at desired height. Insert toothpick to secure Styrofoam pieces together.

2 Apply white glue to plastic leaves and wrap around Styrofoam.

3 Trim off excess leaves.

4 Cover top of Styrofoam with brown clay.

5 Using white glue, attach #18 gauge wires to flower and insert into Styrofoam with leaves. Add vines and other decorations as desired.

Pear

& Apple

TOOLS & SPECIAL MATERIALS

Fruits:
Roller
Styrofoam Balls
Scissors
DECO Detail Stick (Round)
Toothpick

Paint and Assembly:
Paint
Brush (#6 and #12)
Semi-Gloss Varnish
Palette
Styrofoam
Moss Sheet
#18 Gauge Wire
White Glue

PEAR AND APPLE

PEAR AND APPLE

1 Roll out 3-inch diameter clay to ¹/₈-inch thick.

2 Wrap clay around 3-inch diameter Styrofoam ball and gather excess to make top portion.

3 Stretch top portion to create pear shape.

4 Smooth and squeeze neck area.

5 Cut top portion and smooth edges with hand.

6 Creates grooves by using round DECO detail stick.

7 Cover 2-inch diameter Styrofoam ball with clay and shape into apple with hands and fingers. Use knuckle to make a dent at top of the apple.

8 To make stem, cover toothpick with brown clay.

PAINT AND ASSEMBLY

9 Pull clay to the bottom to create stem.

10 Make 1-inch long stem and let dry.

11 Insert stem into top of pear and apple.

1 Color pear and apple using different combinations of white gesso, yellow, orange, green, brown and red. Finish with varnish.

2 Cut Styrofoam to desired shape. Apply white glue to moss sheet and attach to Styrofoam sides. Cut excess.

3 Cover top with orange clay. Using white glue, attach #18 gauge wire to dried fruits and flowers. Arrange as desired.

4 Fill gaps with smaller flowers and fillers.

Christmas

Stocking

TOOLS & SPECIAL MATERIALS

DECO Detail Stick (Angled)
Roller
Mold A
White Glue

STOCKING

STOCKING

1 Make one 4-inch diameter ball. Split ball into one-third (small) and two-third (large) pieces. Roll small clay to 1/8-inch thick and large clay to 3/16-inch thick.

2 Use angled DECO detail stick to cut stocking shape out of larger clay. Trace stocking shape onto smaller clay, and remove excess.

3 Stack stocking with thicker piece on top. Leave top portion open.

4 Apply "band" to top portion, covering about one-third of stocking.

5 Place thin rope to add accent.

6 To create leaves, make small teardrop and press onto mold A.

7 Attach leaves and add teardrops to the middle. Use white glue if clay is not holding. Insert finger to open top portions.

8 Decorate as desired, using white glue to secure.

Reindeer with Christmas Tree

TOOLS & SPECIAL MATERIALS

REINDEER:
Stem (see pg. 13)
Water Glue
White Glue
DECO Detail Stick (Round)
Toothpick
Plastic Texture Brush
Pin
#24 Gauge Wire

CHRISTMAS TREE:
Stem (see pg. 13)
Texture Brush
#18 Gauge Wire
#26 Gauge Wire
Scissors
Water Glue
White Glue
Glitter
Brush

REINDEER WITH CHRISTMAS TREE

REINDEER

1 Make one 1-inch, ½-inch, 2-inch, and 2 ½-inch diameter balls. Make one 8-inch long brown stem (see page 13). Dry completely and cut stem into four 2-inch long pieces.

2 Use water glue to attach small portion of tan colored clay onto stems to create legs. Flatten bottoms.

3 Roll 2 ½-inch diameter clay to form body shape.

4 Apply white glue to tip of legs and insert into body. Straighten legs to ensure it will stand.

5 Add small amount clay where legs and body meet.

6 Smooth areas with finger.

7 Use part of 2-inch ball and attach to front of the body to create neck. If clay starts to dry, use a drop of water or water glue to adhere together.

8 Use ½-inch diameter ball to mold head with fingers.

9 Attach ears and smooth to blend with head.

10 Take lighter colored clay and make into a ½-inch ball. Flatten and wrap around nose.

REINDEER

11 Break toothpick in half and insert into neck. Attach head to other end of toothpick.

12 Smooth neck and head area to connect separation. If clay starts to dry, use a drop of water glue or water to adhere together.

13 Insert lighter colored clay into each ear to add accents. Decorate face with nose and eyes and add a tail.

14 Make two horns using lighter colored clay and let them dry.

15 Insert one end of #24 gauge wire into horn and other end into the head. Use white glue to secure both ends.

16 Roll out two different colored clays. Place palms at end. Twist clay, moving one hand forward and the other back, two or three times to make rope tight.

17 Flatten clay to about 5-inches long.

18 Use plastic brush to add texture. Wrap clay around neck to create scarf.

19 Create tiny poinsettias by rolling small teardrops.

20 Flatten edges of teardrops with fingers.

CHRISTMAS TREE

21 Use tip of long pin to create veins.

22 Use either water or white glue to attach petals to body. Tip of pin can be used to apply pressure.

23 Add three tiny teardrops to the centers of poinsettias. Continue other decorations as desired.

1 To create tree, make brown stem (see page 13). Be sure base gradually tapers to tree tip. Let dry completely and cut stem to desired height.

2 Make teardrop shape and flatten with palm of hand.

3 Use texture brush to create lines.

4 Randomly cut long and short slits to create tree leaves.

5 Make variety of sizes. Apply glue to one end of #26 gauge wire and insert into leaf. Let dry.

6 Apply white glue to end of wire and insert into stem of tree.

7 Continue adding leaves to fill out tree and add star on top if desired.

8 Add glitter by mixing with water glue and brush gently onto leaves.

BABY SHOWER - SHOES
For Shoes Model on Page 42

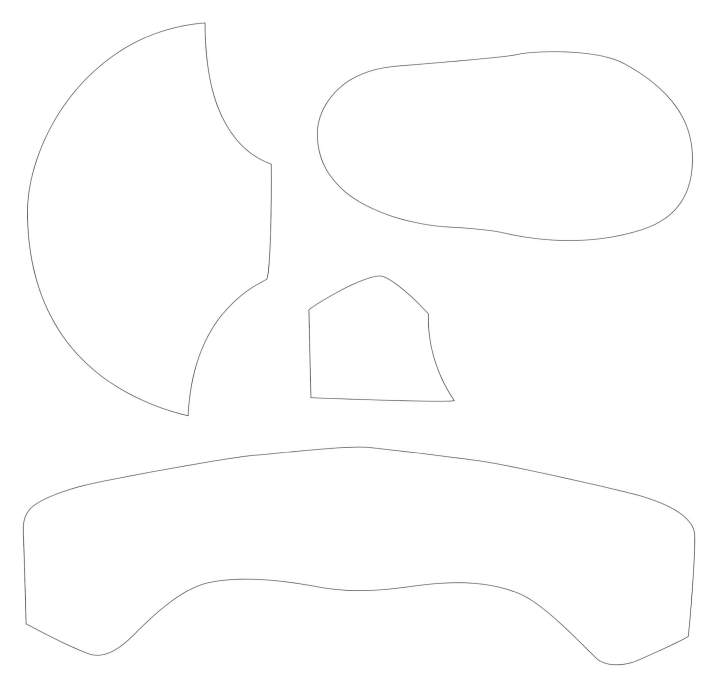

ABY SHOWER - BUTTERFLY
· Card Model on Page 44

LL - LEAF
· Centerpiece Model on Page 73

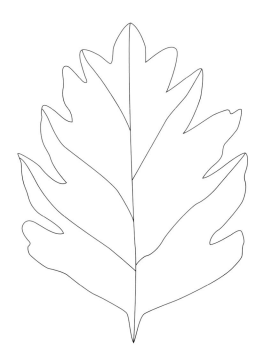